Anthony of Padua

Wonder Worker

1195–1231
Born in Lisbon, Portugal
Feast Day: June 13
Family Connection:
Infants and Pregnant Mothers

Text by Barbara Yoffie
Illustrated by Katherine A. Borgatti

Liguori

Dedication

To my family:
my parents Jim and Peg,
my husband Bill,
our son Sam and daughter-in-law Erin,
and our precious grandchildren
Ben, Lucas, and Andrew

To all the children I have had the privilege of
teaching throughout the years.

Imprimi Potest:
Harry Grile, CSsR, Provincial
Denver Province, The Redemptorists

Published by Liguori Publications
Liguori, Missouri 63057

To order, visit Liguori.org or call 800-325-9521.

p ISBN 978-0-7648-2291-9
e ISBN 978-0-7648-6910-5

Liguori Publications, a nonprofit corporation, is an apostolate of The
Redemptorists. To learn more about The Redemptorists, visit Redemptorists.com.

Printed in the United States of America
22 21 20 19 18 / 6 5 4 3 2
First Edition

Dear Parents and Teachers:

Saints and Me! is a series of children's books about saints, with six books in each set. The first set, *Saints of North America,* honors holy men and women who blessed and served the land we call home. The second set, *Saints of Christmas,* includes heavenly heroes who inspire us through Advent and Christmas and teach us to love the Infant Jesus.

Saints for Families introduces the virtuous lives of seven saints from different times and places who modeled God's love and charity within and for families. Saint Thérèse of Lisieux felt the love of her family and carried it into her religious community (which included her sisters). Saint Anthony of Padua is the patron of infants and children. Saint John Bosco cared for young, homeless boys, raising them like sons. Saint Thomas More, a father of five, imitated Christ's sacrificial love and devotion to the truth until death. Saints Joachim and Anne became the grandparents of Jesus, raising Mary as a sinless disciple. And Saint Gerard Majella, the patron of pregnant mothers, blessed families with food, knowledge, penances, and healing miracles.

Which saint stood up against a king? Who became a tailor and priest? Which saint is "the little flower?" Who was known for his excellent preaching? Which saints lived before Jesus? Which saint climbed trees, did flips, and turned cartwheels? Find out in the *Saints for Families* set—part of the *Saints and Me!* series—and help your child connect to the lives of the saints.

Introduce your children or students to the *Saints and Me!* series as they:

—READ about the lives of the saints and are inspired by their stories.

—PRAY to the saints for their intercession.

—CELEBRATE the saints and relate to their lives.

John Bosco
1815–1888
Born: Becchi, Italy

Joachim and Anne
First century BC
Born: Nazareth (Joachim) Bethlehem (Anne)

Anthony of Padua
1195–1231
Born: Lisbon, Portugal

Gerard Majella
1726–1755
Born: Muro, Italy

Thérèse of Lisieux
1873–1897
Born: Alençon, France

Thomas More
1478–1535
Born: London, England

Long ago in Lisbon, Portugal, a boy named Ferdinand was born. His parents loved him very much. They taught him how to pray and help people. Ferdinand went to school and had lots of friends.

Ferdinand wanted to be a priest. He loved to study, pray, and read the Bible. The Bible was his favorite book. When he was fifteen, he joined the Augustinian order.

Several years later, Ferdinand
met some Franciscan friars. Their
lives were very simple. They told
him how they loved and served
God. "We preach about God.
Our missionaries go to different
countries," they said.

"I think God is calling me to be
a missionary," Ferdinand told the
friars. He left the Augustinian
order and joined the Franciscans.
His new name was Anthony, and
he began wearing a brown habit.
Soon, he and another friar set sail
for Morocco, in Africa.

"I will preach the Good News of Jesus," he told people on the ship. He was very excited. But soon after he arrived, Anthony got sick. He was weak and had a fever. "You are not well. I will take you back to Portugal to rest," said a friend.

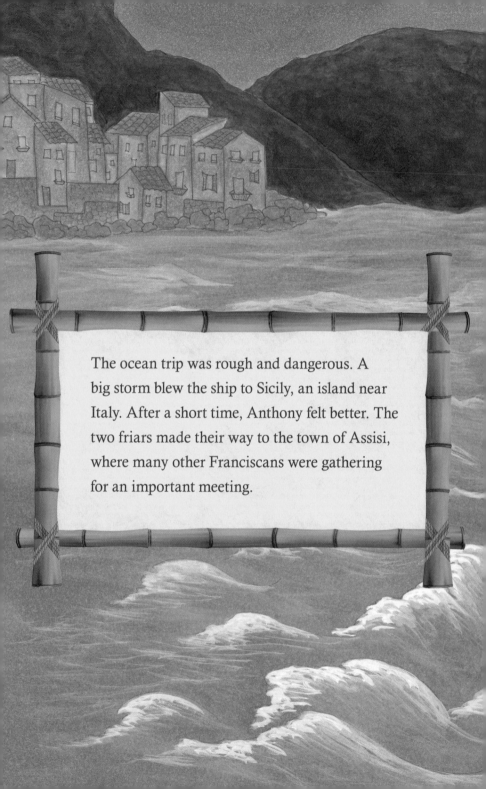

The ocean trip was rough and dangerous. A
big storm blew the ship to Sicily, an island near
Italy. After a short time, Anthony felt better. The
two friars made their way to the town of Assisi,
where many other Franciscans were gathering
for an important meeting.

All the Franciscan friars prayed together and talked about new ideas. When the meeting was over, Anthony went to live in a small hermitage. It was peaceful there. Anthony had lots of time to pray and think about God. Sometimes he helped the other friars in the kitchen or in the garden.

One day the friars went to an ordination ceremony. They could not find a preacher. "Anthony, would you please preach for us today?" one friar asked.

Anthony stood up very slowly and looked at all the people. Then he began to speak.

Everyone was surprised—Anthony was a wonderful preacher! "That was the best sermon I ever heard," said the superior. Anthony had a great gift from God. He was sent to preach to people in France and Italy.

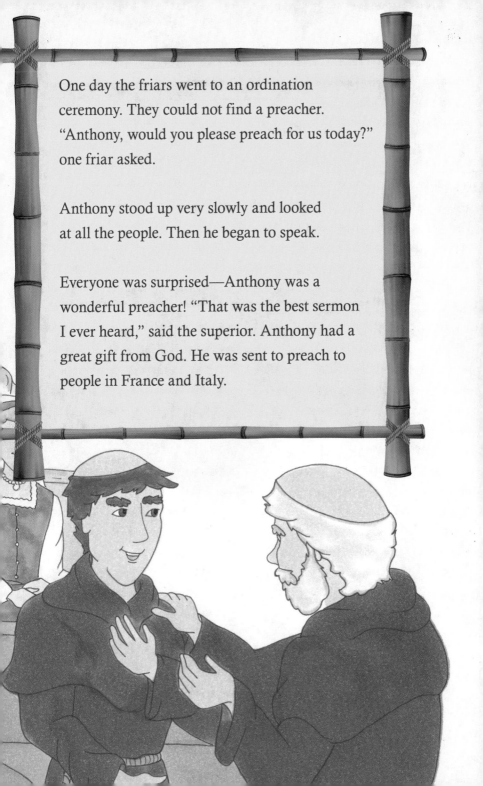

Huge crowds came to hear Anthony. He talked about God and the Church. People learned many things from him. They grew in their faith. Sometimes they even changed their minds and hearts.

A story is told how Anthony even preached to fish! Once, while preaching to a crowd in the city, some people turned and walked away. Anthony walked to the river and preached to the fish instead. When people saw the fish listening to him, they were amazed! "We should listen to Anthony," they cried.

Anthony was asked to teach other Franciscans. He was very busy teaching, preaching, helping the poor, and hearing confessions in many cities. Then he went to the city of Padua in Italy.

Many people in Padua wanted to hear Anthony preach. Sometimes he preached in grassy fields because the church was too small. "Remember the poor. They need our help," begged Anthony. The people of Padua listened to Anthony and changed their selfish ways.

His work in Padua made him very tired. Anthony and two friars traveled to an outdoor retreat. Here, Anthony was able to pray and rest under the shade of walnut trees. One morning he felt very weak. "Please take me back to Padua," he whispered.

They stopped at a convent near Padua. Anthony was too sick to travel. He quietly prayed with the friars. Then he smiled and closed his eyes. Anthony, the great and holy Franciscan preacher, was with God in heaven.

Wonderful stories are told about Saint Anthony. He is called the "Wonder Worker" because miracles happened before and after his death. Tradition tells us that the Infant Jesus appeared to him, and pictures and statues show Saint Anthony holding a young Christ Child. Like Saint Anthony, we can carry the word and love of Jesus into the world.

This is what God asks of you:
Live your faith and share it, too!

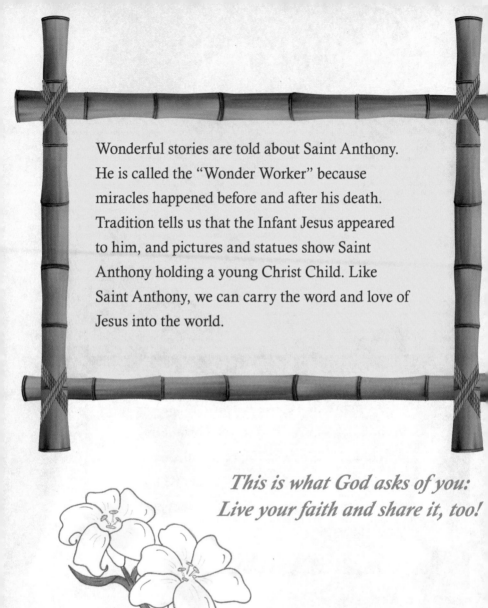

Dear God.

I love You.

Saint Anthony loved You
very much.

He touched many hearts
with his preaching.

Help me to grow
in my faith
and share it
with others.

Amen.

NEW WORDS (Glossary)

Augustinian order: A religious community founded by Saint Augustine

Franciscan order: A religious community founded by Saint Francis of Assisi

Friar: A Franciscan brother who can preach and work outside the monastery where he lives

Hermitage: A quiet place where a religious community lives

Miracle: A wonderful event that cannot be explained and that shows God's love for us

Missionary: A person who teaches the faith or preaches the Gospel in a certain place

Ordination: The ceremony at which a man receives the sacrament of holy orders and becomes a deacon, priest, or bishop

Preacher: A person who teaches about faith, God, and the Good News

Superior: The head or leader of a religious community

****

Saint Anthony of Padua is the patron saint of travelers and the poor, and his help is widely known to assist people in finding lost items. When we keep the saints by our side through the journey of life, we are led to find God's riches and the treasures of heaven.

Liguori Publications
saints and me! series
SAINTS FOR FAMILIES

Collect the entire set!

ANTHONY OF PADUA

wonder worker

JOHN BOSCO

champion for youth

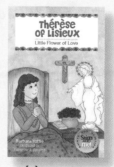

THÉRÈSE OF LISIEUX

Little Flower of Love

JOACHIM AND ANNE

Love for generations

gerard majella

guardian of mothers

Thomas more

faith-filled father

SAINTS FOR FAMILIES ACTIVITY BOOK

Reproducible activites for all 6 books in the series